The Secret *of* Imagining

To Include:

The Secret *of* Causation

&

The Secret *of* Prayer

Neville Goddard

Copyright © 2015 Watchmaker Publishing

ISBN 978-1-60386-675-0

Contents

The Secret *of* Imagining

onight's subject is: "The Secret of Imagining." In almost every particular is the world about us different from what we think it. Why then should we be so incredulous? Life calls on us to believe not less, but more. The secret of imaging is the greatest of all problems, to the solution of which everyone should aspire, for supreme power, supreme wisdom, supreme delight lie in the solution of this mystery.

If you have solved the mystery of imagining you have found Jesus Christ. Jesus Christ is defined for us in scripture as *"The power of God and the wisdom of God."*[1] As we are told in the eighth chapter of the Book of Proverbs, and Wisdom is speaking now, personified as a little child:

"When He laid out the foundation of the world I was beside Him like a little child I was daily His delight, rejoicing before Him always rejoicing in His inhabited world, delighting in the affairs of men.

He who finds me finds life

> *He who misses me injures himself;*
> *All who hate me love death."*

Proverbs 8:29 31, 35, 36

---

[1] First Corinthians 1:24

So find that child that is the symbol of Jesus Christ, who is the creative power and the wisdom of God. Believe me when I tell you that this Jesus Christ of scripture is your own wonderful human imagination. "By him all things were made, and without him was not anything made that was made."[2] He is in the world, and the world was made by Him, and the world knows Him not.

Look into the world and name one thing that wasn't first imagined. You name one thing that does not now exist in your imagination just name it. Name anything in the world that does not now exist in your imagination: "All things exist in the human imagination."[3]

"God is man, and exists in us and we in Him."[4] The eternal abode of man is the imagination; and that is God Himself. Try to disprove it.

God is my pure imagining in myself. He underlies all of my faculties, including perception, but He streams into my surface mind least disguised in the form of productive fancy. I can catch Him in the act of producing these images in my mind. Just try it as you are seated here. Try to think of anything. Try to catch Him in the act of actually producing in your own mind's eye all these images. *"For all things exist in the human imagination."* But how can I single out one and clothe it so that it becomes an objective fact?

That is the secret, for they all exist within me. But how can I catch one and clothe it? Well I will try to show you tonight what I know from my own personal experience. Scripture

---

[2] John 1:3

[3] *"Jerusalem" by* William Blake

[4] *"Annotations to Berkeley" by* William Blake

teaches it, but it tells it in a strange and wonderful way: how to clothe it.

You see this room in which we are now? It's more real now than your own home is to you; yet you know your home more intimately than you know this room. Yet this room, at the moment, while you are in it, is more real than your own home. How different the cubic reality from the plane of any depiction of it. This room is now so "real" because we are in it, and we are all imagination. We're in it; and to us, it's real. Think of your own home. Do we not have the capacity to draw it, to paint it? But in your mind's eye you have a plane depiction of it, but it's not as real now as the room is. This room is real because we're in it.

Now this is what I mean by making something that is only a thought something that is real. How do I do it? I single out, out of my own wonderful human imagination, that which I want to make real. It's all in you. Then I must enter into it as I have entered into this room. "*If the spectator would enter into any one of these images in his imagination, approaching it on the fiery chariot of his own contemplative thought,*"[5] it would become just as real to him as this room.

You may ask, "What would that do to me? Will it become real in the not distant future?" I know from my own experience, it will. You can sit here and enter into a state. It may not take on quite the reality of this room, but it will if you persist in it; it will become just like this. When you open your eyes, it vanishes. But does it mean that I tasted that, and that's all? No. Having gone into it, may I tell you, it will follow you? It will not recede into the past as memory; it will

---

[5] *Visions of the Last Judgment*" by William Blake

advance into the future and you will confront it. This is the secret of imaging, which is finding out the secret of God.

You are an immortal being. You cannot die because you are all imagination. Man is all imagination; and God truly is man; and He exists in us, and we in Him. And that immortal body of man is the human imagination, and that is Jesus Christ Himself, the Eternal Body of man and it cannot die. You cannot die. The body, yes, this will fade; but I am not the garment that I am wearing. I am the wearer of the garment, and the wearer of this garment is all imagination. This is the story that the Bible teaches.

When we read in the Bible: *"I, even I, am He. I kill, and I make alive; I wound, and I heal; and there is no god beside me."*[6] This is not a being outside of you speaking; this is the Being that you really are, speaking within you, trying to persuade Himself of His own wonderful power to create. It can kill, and yet it can make alive. It can resurrect from the dead. And that is your own wonderful human imagination.

The day will come; you will taste this power that you possess. You will come into a room just like this, and you will still it not by commanding anyone in the room to be still. Leave them just as they are. But you will arrest within yourself an activity that you feel, and as you still it in you, everything that you observe becomes still perfectly still. You could go forward and examine them, and they are dead. Everything is perfectly still and dead. The life is in you. You release the activity, and they once more become animated and continue to do what they intended to do. You could, when you stilled the activity within you, change their motivation; and

---

[6] Deuteronomy 32:39

when you release it, they will do entirely different from what they intended to do prior to your arrestment within you of that activity.

"As the Father has life in Himself, He has granted the Son also to have life in Himself"[7]; and you have that within you. You're not quite aware of it yet, but you will become aware. Those that I am teaching will have dreams, as you have dreams; and in their dreams they will become awake, and then arrest it in the dream and change the motivation and see the intended act change.

Here is one. A friend became aware that she was dreaming, and here's a man who intended to hurt her. He got out of the car and came towards her, and she became afraid; and her fright woke her; but instead of waking on the bed, she awoke in the dream. Then she realized, "This is what he teaches. Now I will simply arrest it." She didn't argue with him; she arrested, within her, the activity that animated him. And she said to him, "You are tired. You need a good hot cup of coffee and then a good sound sleep," and then she told him exactly what he needed, and released the activity within her. He shook his head as though something strange had happened within him, and he got back into the car all in her dream and drove off. You see, she changed his intention towards her.

This may seem impossible to the world. As I started this lecture, almost everything in this world is so completely unlike what it appears to be. And I am telling you from my own experience; I am not speculating. I am not theorizing. The power of which I speak is a power within you. That power is not something on the outside; it's your own wonderful human

---

[7] John 5:26

imagination, and you will learn to control it. Your imagination animates the world in which you live. You change your imagination, and you change the world.

To attempt to change circumstances before I change my own imaginal activity is to struggle against the very nature of my own being, for my own imaginal activity is animating my world. If I believe that I am injured or that others are against me, I have conjured them in my world, and they have to be against me. If I fully believe that all are working towards the fulfillment of my good, they have to work towards the fulfillment of my good. I don't ask them. I don't compel them. I simply do it only within myself, and the whole vast world exists within me. Therefore, it is myself "pushed out." It's objectified. I don't have to change affairs; I only change it within myself; and then everyone, though I know him or not by name, it doesn't really matter, it's myself "pushed out."

I couldn't tell you the atoms of my body, but it is my body. I couldn't tell you if you took the hand off, that it's my hand I am looking at, any more than I could tell you your name or anything about you; yet, you are myself "pushed out," as this body is the body I wear. And so, as the body obeys my mind, you my "pushed out" body will obey my mind too. All I have to do is to concern myself with what I want in this world, and try to keep it within the frame of the Golden Rule: doing unto others only that which I would want done unto me, nothing more than that; hurting no one, doing not a thing to anyone other than that which I would want done unto me.

If you want all the lovely things done, do only the lovely, and do it all in your own wonderful human imagination. Then you will realize this tremendous secret of imaging. It is the greatest of all secrets, to the solution of which everyone in the world should aspire, because Christ is the answer.

Christ is defined for us in the first chapter of First Corinthians as "the power of God and the wisdom of God."[8] Here is the power of God and the wisdom of God; and I have found the power to be in myself.

"*You mean, Christ is in me?*" Are we not taught that in scripture? "Know ye not that Jesus Christ is in you? Do you not know that Jesus Christ is in you, unless of course you fail to meet the test?"[9] Well then, test it. How would I test it?

A friend of mine, maybe, is unwell; or maybe he's unemployed, or maybe he is not earning enough to meet the obligations of life. All right, he is in me. As I think of him, he's in me. He need not be physically present for me to think of him; he's in me. I think of him; I conjure him. Well, can I change his entire picture in me? I assume that he is talking to me, and he's telling me that he has never had more, he has never felt better; and as I believe in what I am seeing in my own mind's eye, I believe in him. That is Christ in me, and all things are possible to Christ. Well then, test it and see if it works. See if you do not see him in the not distance future earning more, looking better; and everything in the world that you have done within you, he responds to. He need not praise you or thank you. You don't need his praise; you don't need his thanks. You don't need confirmation from him, other than he does conform to what you have done in yourself concerning him.

---

[8] First Corinthians 1:24
[9] Second Corinthians 13:5

You ask no one to thank you. Thank nothing. You are simply exercising the power of God within you. "And the power of God and the wisdom of God is Jesus Christ."[10] And there is nothing in the world but God. It is all God in you "pushed out," and God is your own wonderful human imagination. He can't be closer. God is never so far off as even to be near, for nearness implies separation. He's not separated. God actually, literally became as I am, that I may be as He is. He is not something on the outside. No matter how near He is, He can't even touch me. He actually became me, with all of my weaknesses, all of my limitations; and now I am trying to struggle within myself to find out who I am, and that's His name. My name is in Him. What's your name? "Go and say I AM has sent you." "Is that your name?" "Yes, forever and forever it is my name." "What name? Jehovah?" "No." "The Lord?" "No, I AM." That's His name. That is His name forever and forever.

Well I cannot say, "I am," and point elsewhere. I can't say, "I am," and feel something is near me. It can't even be near. Something can be near to what I am, but "I AM" can't be near. And that's the name of God forever and forever. So you are the Lord Jesus Christ.

Now a pattern is given to us in scripture by which you will know that you are; and I promise you, from my own personal experience, that you shall have it. It is a true story. The truest story ever told is the story of the Lord Jesus Christ. When He said, "I am the Father," may I tell you, if he's a father, he has a son, hasn't he? Or at least he has a child; but I tell you, it's a son. He said, "When you see me, you see the Father"; but if I

---

[10] First Corinthians 1:24

look at you and I say, "Well then, you are the father, show me your son." He can't show me His son outside as His son, because He and I are one. He has to show me His son not of blood nor of the will of the flesh; it has to be born, not of blood nor of the will of the flesh nor of the will of man, but of God. And He tells me that He is God, and He tells me that *He and I are one.* Well then, it can't be born in any normal, natural way. He has to be born of God.

Well then, who is your son? He tells me in scripture that David calls Him, "Father."

"David calls you, 'Father'?"

"Yes." He said, "I inspired the prophets," and read the Prophets; and in the Prophets, David calls the Lord, "my Father."

"You mean David, then, is my son?"

"Yes, he's my son."

"But I do not know him," you will say.

But I will tell you, from my own personal experience, you will know it because I know it; David called me, "my Father." David called me, "my Lord." David called me the Rock of his salvation. Everything that is said in scripture concerning what he said of the Lord, he said of me. And so, I stood, and here is David, and I knew it beyond all doubt that here is my son, and my son is David, not a David, the David the only David the David of biblical fame. And as he called me, "Father," memory returned.

So God actually became me, and then He unfolds Himself within me. Well, as He unfolds Himself within me, it's only the memory of God that He gave up in order to become me. He had to completely give up all that was God to become this little witness that is called a man called Neville. So when His memory returns and He became me, it is my memory returning. He actually gave me Himself as He gave you Himself; and the day will come as He unfolds Himself within you, your memory returns because it's God's memory returning. He completely empties Himself in order to become you.

This is the story of the Christian faith; the fulfillment of all the promises made in the Old Testament. The Old Testament is only a prophetic blueprint of the life of Jesus Christ. It's an adumbration, a foreshadowing in a not altogether conclusive or immediately evident way; but as it unfolds within you, it's nothing more than God's memory returning. But having become you, it becomes your memory returning, and you awaken as God Himself. And there is nothing in the world like God.

Now you ask, what, all the horrors of the world, the pain, the suffering? Yes. It takes all the "furnaces" to prepare you to receive the gift that He gives, and the gift is Himself. God actually became you. He gave Himself to you, that you may be God. And God in you is your own wonderful human imagination, that's God.

Now tonight try it. I ask you to believe me. But whether you believe me or not, try it anyway. Take a friend of yours and bring him before your mind's eye, and then talk to him from the premise of your desire for him fulfilled not going to be, but already fulfilled. And having done it, believe that all things are possible to the Lord Jesus Christ; and you just saw Jesus Christ in action, for you saw the creative power of God in action, and that's Jesus Christ. That is your own wonderful human imagination.

Now believe in the reality of what you've just done. Believe that this subjective appropriation of your objective hope for a friend is a fact. That is really praying. And all things are possible to God. Go within and appropriate it just completely appropriate it, and see it unfold within your own vast marvelous world.

So this wonderful secret is the secret of the Lord Jesus Christ. If you turn on the outside and turn to another, you do not know the Lord Jesus Christ. You can make all kinds of images of Him. That's not the Lord Jesus Christ. If any man should ever come and say, "Look, there he is," or "Here he is," don't believe it. Why? Because when you actually meet Him, you are going to meet your Self. The Christ of faith comes to us as one unknown; yet one who in some ineffable mystery lets us experience who He is; and when we experience Jesus Christ, we experience Him in the first person, singular, present tense experience. You will never see Him coming from without. Let no one tell you you're going to meet Him coming from without. You will meet Him awakening Himself within you as you. That's the Lord Jesus Christ. That's the great sacrifice. He is crucified on Humanity.

Every human form is the cross that He wears; and in that form He awakens as the one in whom He awakens. He awakens as that Being, and that Being is the Lord Jesus Christ. And because He is the father of David, David called that Being, "Father"; then you know, "I am He."

Oh, I can tell you from now to the ends of time, and I may not persuade you to believe it; but when it happens to you, you need no further persuasion, for you are confronted with the facts and there you stand in the presence of you own son, and the son is the Son of God.

"*I will tell of the decree of the Lord,*" said David. "He said unto me, '*Thou art my son. Today I have begotten thee.*'"[11] These are the words of David in the Second Psalm. "I will tell of the decree of the Lord. He said unto me, 'Thou art my son.'" That son is going to call you, "Father"; and then, and only then, you will know you are God the Father. That is the mystery of the entire world. And so, what you accomplish in this world concerning finances is wonderful for you as an individual in the world of Caesar. What you do concerning the social world all these things it's marvelous; but you will only really fulfill your destiny as you fulfill scripture, for the purpose of life is to fulfill scripture.

"I have accomplished the work Thou gavest me to do." What work? All that the prophets spoke about me; and beginning with Moses and the prophets and the Psalms; he interpreted to them in all the scriptures the things concerning Himself. Then said he, "Scripture must be fulfilled in you," and the purpose of life is to fulfill scripture the prophecy of God to man, for He gave man Himself, or promised to give man Himself. And He promised me a son. The son He promised was His Son; and in giving me His Son, He gave me Himself, for His Son calls me, "Father." And that is the whole mystery of life. There's nothing but God. One Being expanding Himself forever and forever and forever, each Himself. And even though he calls you, "Father," may I tell you, you will not lose your identity. You are individualized and you will tend towards ever greater and greater individualization. And yet, you are the Father of my son; and if you are the Father of my son, then you and I are one. It is a great mystery, we are

---

[11] Psalm 2:7

brothers, for you do not lose your identity and I do not lose my identity. So you and I, behind these masks are eternal brothers the Father of the One and only Begotten Son.

Well if you are the father of my son, and my own wife is the "father" of my son, then the relationship on earth of men, or friend to friend and wife to husband, is above this level, and we are eternal brothers, all forming the one Father.

So tonight, you take me seriously; and when you go home or start it here, you put into practice this greatest of all secrets; the secret of imaging. There is no greater secret in the world. Every child born of woman is alive because it was imagined. And imaging is God in action. That's the soul of man imaging; and that is the power of God. And the power of God is Christ. And that is the wisdom of God, and the wisdom of God is Christ.

A child can imagine. Well, that's Christ. That is Christ crucified on that little tiny garment, and it suffers with everything that that little child imagines, or it enjoys with everything the little child imagines. It wears all the stripes and all the blows that man in his misuse of that power will do. He doesn't criticize him. He waits upon me as indifferently and as quickly when the will in me is evil as when it is good. That way, He bears all my stripes. He bears all of my misuse of His power, knowing that in the end, I will awaken and use it only lovingly.

When I completely awaken from the dream of life, I will use this creative power of God only lovingly. But in the meantime while I am trying to awaken to the use of this power, I misuse it. And may I tell you, you will confront this vision, and you will see what you did from the beginning, for you didn't begin it a few years ago in your mother's womb. You have been coming through the centuries.

One night, here I saw this monstrous creature covered in hair. It looked like a gorilla, and the hair was all dark brown from head to toe. It was a monster. And here, the most glorious, heavenly creature a female; and this was a male monster. And it called out to this heavenly creature, "Mother, mother." Well, I knew this could not be this radiant, heavenly creature; and so I struck him. And as I struck it, it gloated; it loved violence. And I pummeled it, and it gloated all the more. Well, it could speak in a guttural tone, calling this heavenly being, "Mother." And that annoyed me. Then suddenly from within me I knew. Why, this is my own creation. And so is this one. They are only the outpicturing of my two different uses of the creative power that I am.

Here (the monster) is the complete embodiment of every misused moment of my life. Every time I was violent, I created and fed this monster. It whispered in my ear to be monstrous, to be violent, to be bad, to be evil, for it fed only on this thought. And here (the heavenly creature) was the embodiment of all my loving thoughts. Every kind, considerate, wonderful thought in my life fed this one.

As I saw this monstrous thing and realized that it was my own offspring, it was the fruit of my misspent energy, I pledged myself. There was no one to whom I could turn, I pledged myself that if it took eternity I would redeem it. It did not come into being through any power other than my own misuse of my own power. It could not have been brought into being; and that thing could not live, and it could not help itself. I didn't condemn it.

At that moment, I felt compassion beyond the wildest dreams of anyone for this monstrous thing that I had created. And when I made myself that pledge that I would redeem it if it took me eternity, at that very moment, the whole thing got smaller and smaller and smaller; but it didn't waste the energy that it embodied returned to me. I began to feel a power that, until that moment, I had never felt before. And this one began to grow. The beauty that she embodied and personified glowed as the energy came back from this one (the monster) to me; and the whole thing dissolved before my eyes.

So, "nothing is lost in all my holy mountain" I did not lose that energy that I misplaced, it returned to me, that was embodied in that monster. And throughout the centuries, it was it who whispered in my ear monstrous things to be done, because it could only feed on violence. It could only feed on evil.

Then I realized what it meant: that I ate of the Tree of the Knowledge of Good and Evil. And so it fed upon evil, and she fed upon the good. And then the evil that was only the energy misspent returned to me; and then the whole thing came back to me. And then I broke the spell, and I awoke in this world.

Well everyone is going to confront that gorilla on the threshold. Everyone has him, unseen by mortal eye, and he whispers into your ear to entertain the unlovely thoughts of the world. And your every reaction that is unlovely, it feeds upon it; and your every thought that is kind and wonderful and loving, she feeds upon it. And the day will come, you will be strong enough to confront this. And may I tell you, it will take you the twinkling of a second to dissolve it? You don't labor upon it. All it needs is the core of integrity within you. When you pledge yourself, and no one else, you don't swear upon your mother, you don't swear upon a friend, you don't swear upon the Bible; you pledge yourself to redeem it. At the moment you pledge yourself, and within you, you know you mean it, the whole thing dissolves. It's no time at all in dissolving. And then all the energy returns to you, and you are stronger than ever before to go forward now and eat of the Tree of the Knowledge of Good and Evil.

And if you forward and misuse it again, you start another form building; and one day you will dissolve it again. Eventually you will become completely awakened, and you will use your wonderful power only not for good, that tree will come to an end, for Life itself. For eating of the Tree of the Knowledge of Good and Evil is this world. The day will come that you will eat of the Tree of Life that bears the fruit of truth and error. Error will embody itself here, and one day you will confront the error, and the error will dissolve before your mind's eye as truth begins to glow before you, because you are eating, then, of the Tree of Life as you formally ate of the Tree of the Knowledge of Good and Evil. And the combat of good and evil produces this monster, and the combat of truth and error produces an entirely different form of being, more glorious than that one of good and more horrible than this. The error will dissolve just as quickly when you confront error.

So if today your teaching is not true and you live by it, you are building something just as monstrous; but one day you will confront error and you will discover that you lived by a false concept of God something on the outside of Self; that you formerly worshiped a little golden figure made of gold and silver. It had eyes, but could not see. It had ears, but could not hear. It had a mouth, but could not speak. It had feet, and it could not walk. It made no sound within its throat. And those who made it are just like it. And those who trusted it are just like it too.

So all the little icons in the world that people worship these are the little things called "error"; and one day you will discover the true God. And when you discover the true God, you will find that He is all within your own wonderful being as your own wonderful human imagination. You'll walk in the consciousness of being God. You don't brag about it.

As Blake answered when they asked him, "What do you think of Jesus Christ?" Blake answered, "Jesus Christ is the only God"; but he hastened to add to it, "But so am I, and so are you."

So you don't tell anyone. You simply know that you are the Being spoken of in scripture as "God the Father." For all that is said of Him, you are going to experience; and you are going to experience it in the first person, singular, and a present tense experience. And then you will know.

Today is the eleventh year since it happened to me right here in this city, right across the way at the hotel with the star at the top of the roof, the Sir Francis Drake, on the 20th day of July 1959. It was then that I, at 4:00 in the morning, felt within my head the most intense vibration, and I thought, this is a brain hemorrhage, and this is it. I knew nothing of the human form, and I thought I cannot possible survive what I am feeling; so this must be what they call a massive brain hemorrhage. But instead of departing this world, I awoke to find myself within my own skull; and I knew that I was entombed completely within my own skull. I was fully awake, as I've never been awake before, and here I am sealed the skull is sealed, and I am in it. The skull is not a little thing like this (indicating the head). It's the size of a huge, big sepulcher, and

I knew it to be my skull. I also know intuitively that I could get out by pushing the base of my skull. As I pushed it, a stone rolled away, and I saw the little opening, and I put my head through it and pushed; and I came out, inch by inch, just as a child is born from the mother's womb. But instead of being born from below of flesh and blood, I was "born from above" out of the skull Golgotha, where Christ was buried. But it was not another coming out, I am coming out. There was no other. I had no companion in that skull. I myself was there, and I came out. And when I looked back at the body out of which I came, it was ghastly pale, turning its head from side to side like one in recovery from a great ordeal. I stood up and looked at it, and then suddenly I heard this strange, strange wind this unearthly wind that I had heard in the tomb within my head, well now, it seemed to be divided and coming from the corner of the room.

As I looked over to see if it really came from that side, and I looked back three or four seconds later the body had been removed. There is no body; but in its place sat my three older brothers. My eldest sat where the head was, my second one sat where the right foot was, and the third one sat where the left foot was; and they heart this same unearthly wind. They couldn't see me. I not only saw them, I could read their thoughts as I could read my own. Their thoughts all were objective to me. Everything was objective. They couldn't have an emotion that wasn't objective. They couldn't have a thought that wasn't objective. And yet, I heard their voices.

And then my brother Lawrence got off the bed and started towards the same direction that I thought this wind originated this peculiar wind. As he took one or two steps, he said, "Why, it's Neville's baby. This is the cause of this peculiar, unearthly wind."

My brother Victor and my brother Cecil, they said, "How can Neville have a baby?"

He didn't argue the point. He lifted from the floor a little infant wrapped in swaddling clothes and brought it and placed it on the bed; and I took that infant up into my arms, and as I looked into its face and said, "How is my sweetheart," this little heavenly face broke into the most glorious smile; and then the whole scene dissolved.

There was the resurrection from the dead, followed by the "birth from above." So we are "born from above," as told us in the Book of Peter. "We are born anew through the resurrection of Jesus Christ from the dead."[12] There is only one Being resurrected, the Being who descended into man; and that is Jesus Christ. He descended into man, the power of God and the wisdom of God, and united with man; and when they became one and fulfilled the destiny of that Being, only He now wakes as you. And so, you awake as the Lord Jesus Christ, without loss of identity.

So eleven years ago on the 20th day of July, back in 1959 here in this city, that drama took place within me. So it is my birthday today in a spiritual sense. The little body that now stands before you, that came in the year 1905. It will depart and turn into dust; but that which awoke within me is the Immortal Self that cannot die. And those who have not had the experience, that Immortal Self is still there, and it cannot die. You will be restored to life in a world just like this to

---

[12] First Peter 1:3

continue the drama until that experience that I've just told you takes place within you.

Nothing dies. The little rose that bloomed once, blooms forever. It turns to ash as the body will turn to ash, but you the Immortal You, who is all imagination cannot die. But it will awaken one day in the same manner that it awoke within me. It was buried in Golgotha, which means "the skull." He is buried on Calvary, which is the skull. It is in the skull of man that God is buried; and there *God-in-man* will awake.

So here this night you put it to the test as you are challenged in scripture to test Him. And you test, not another, you test your own wonderful human imagination, for that is the Lord Jesus Christ.

The truest story ever told is the story of Jesus Christ. Let the world rise in opposition and say there is no Lord. As Blake brought out so beautifully in his poem "Jerusalem":

". . . *Babel mocks; saying there is no God or Son of God; That Thou, O Human Imagination, O Divine Body of the Lord Jesus Christ art all A delusion; but I know Thee, O Lord, when Thou arisest upon My weary eyes, even in this dungeon and this iron mill. . . For Thou also sufferest with me, although I behold Thee not.*

. . . . *And the Divine Voice answers,*

. . . . *Fear not. Lo, I am with you always, Only believe in me, that I have the power to raise from death Thy Brother who sleepeth in Albion.*"

You can't get away from your own imagination. You can't get away from it because that's your own being. That is the reality. But it suffers with you. He is the Lord Jesus Christ within you. Now test Him tonight. Test Him for the good. Do you want a better job when they say they are letting people out? Forget what the papers say. Forget what anything says. "All things are possible to the Lord Jesus Christ."[13]

If you don't have enough money, forget what the paper says, you assume that you have it. "All things are possible to God." He sets no limits whatsoever on the power of believing. Can you believe it? Well try to believe it. Try to believe, first of all, in God. Well God is your own imagination. Well believe in Him; that whatever you can imagine is possible.

Can you imagine that you have now the kind of a job that you want? The income that would come from it? The fun in the doing of the work? Well then walk as though it were true; and to the best of your ability believe that it's true. And that assumption though denied by your senses, though the world would say it is false; if you persist in it, it will harden into fact.

This is the law of your own wonderful imaging. Believe it, and it will become a reality.

---

[13] Matthew 19:26

The Secret *of* Causation

"The secret of imagining is the greatest of all problems, to the solution of which every man should aspire; for supreme power, supreme wisdom, and supreme delight, lie in the solution of this great mystery." Imagination is the Jesus Christ of scripture, and when you solve the great mystery of imagining, you will have found the cause of the phenomena of life. Imagination is called "Jehovah" in the Old Testament and "Jesus" in the New, but they are one and the same being. Divine Imagination, containing all, reproduces itself in the human imagination; therefore, all things exist in the human imagination. When you solve the problem of imagining, you will have found Jesus Christ, the secret of causation.

Let me share with you two experiences which came to me this past week. The first lady said: "Returning from a wonderful cruise recently, I checked my baggage at La Guardia Airport, bound for Chicago, where I expected to spend a few days with friends. Arriving in Chicago, I discovered that the bag which contained most of my clothes and all of the presents I had bought for my friends and relatives – as well as a locket I had had made from the engagement and wedding band my late husband had given me – was missing. I immediately reported the loss to the airline, but when I arrived in California there was still no trace of it.

"A week later I received a letter saying that the bag could not be located, and my first reaction was to curse the airline for their negligence; but then I remembered that imagining creates reality. I tried to reconstruct the letter, but when I couldn't feel its words were true, I began to assume that the bag had arrived at the house. I lifted it up on the bed, opened it, put my clothes away, as well as the gifts which were there. I did this every night and during the day, when I would notice my thoughts going astray.

"When the grandchildren would ask about their presents, I told them that they were on their way, as I never admitted to anyone that the bag was lost. How could I, if I believe what I had imagined? Six weeks later I received a letter from the airline saying: `If you do not pick up your bag within five days, you will be charged storage.' I picked up the bag to find everything there, and put them all away, just as I had imagined doing." Then the lady added this thought: "Love's labor is never lost. Everything in that bag was loved, and I knew that if this principle was true, it would prove itself in the testing – and it did."

I can't thank her enough for sharing this experience with me, that I, in turn, may share it with you. Everything is created by the human imagination. There is no other God. You can use your imagination wisely and create a heaven here on earth, or use it foolishly and create the world's havoc; but there is only one power, called the Lord God Jehovah in the Old Testament, and Jesus Christ in the New.

This lady's first impulse was to curse the person who stupidly lost the bag. Then, remembering what she had heard, she tried to revise the letter. When that didn't seem natural, she asked herself what she would do if the bag was now in her possession. Assuming it was there, she did everything she would do if it was a physical fact – and six weeks later it was.

That is what I mean by imagining creating reality, for an assumption is faith; and without faith it is impossible to please your own wonderful human imagination. Divine Imagination, containing all, reproduces itself in human imagination; therefore, the human imagination contains all. The world is the human imagination pushed out. Not knowing this, man cheats himself, murders himself, declares war against himself, and does all sorts of evil against himself; but do not let yourself be intimidated by the horror of the world. Leave it alone, for it is only the misuse of the power exercised by sleeping mankind.

Now, another lady shared this experience with me: She found herself in a neighbor's kitchen, filled with men and women dressed as Mennonites. (You all know what the Mennonite look like. Originating in Zurich, Switzerland in the year 1525, they moved into Germany, France, Belgium, and Holland, to finally arrive in this country in the 17th century. Now numbering around 150,000 to 200,000, they continue to dress and live in the same fashion they did when they arrived here 300 years ago. Here is a fixed belief which has perpetuated itself year after year.)

The neighbor's second husband had mistreated her, so the Mennonites killed him. Although she tried to tell them that it was wrong to take the life of another, as far as they were concerned it was the right thing to do. He had joined their society and knew their laws, which stated that if a man mistreated a woman, he was to be killed. No matter what argument she used, she could not persuade them that what they had done was wrong.

In the 16th chapter of the Book of Proverbs you will read: "All the ways of a man are pure in his own eyes, but God weighs the heart. God has made everything for its purpose, even the wicked for the day of trouble." Believing in an eye for an eye and a tooth for a tooth, they felt no remorse or guilt for their actions, for in their eyes it was perfect.

Suddenly a limousine appeared and men dressed in black and carrying machine guns entered the house. As she watched, the leader, pointing his gun at the lady, ordered the others to search the house. Then the lady awoke, not to find herself on her bed, but standing in the room of her dream. Suddenly realizing that she was awake in her dream and the action was taking place within her, she stopped the activity, which allowed her to see anyone as alive and independent of her perception, and they all froze.

(As Blake said, "*All that you behold, though it appears without, it is within, in your human imagination of which this world of mortality is but a shadow*.")

Turning to the leader she said: "You don't want to kill her, you love her and she loves you." Then turning to the woman she said, "You love him and he loves you." Allowing them to obey her will, she stood back and watched, as the man put his gun down and – with outstretched arms – moved to embrace the woman. Turning to go into the kitchen and release the animation there, her alarm caused her to awaken to this level of her dream.

This world is just as much a dream as that one, but man is sound asleep and does not know that he is dreaming. No one will sentence a man for dreaming he killed another; rather they will try to analyze it for him, and most of our so-called experts on dreams are past masters of misinterpretation. They do not realize the great mystery surrounding us. I tell you: the whole vast world is the individual dreamer pushed out, and the conflict is within himself, and not on the outside.

This lady's drama began as something taking place on the outside, and seemingly independent of her perception of it. Then she awoke to an activity within her, which was animating and making alive all that she perceived. Arresting it, everyone became frozen, like statues. She changed their intentions, then watched as they were reanimated once more — but now bewildered, because of the radical change in them which took place in her.

Scripture calls this repentance, or metanoia, which means "a radical change of mind." When ideas change, so do your intentions and attitude towards life. The story is told, that at his trial, the Risen Christ said to the symbol of the authority of this world: "You have no power over me, were it not given you from above." This world is a drama which has been set in motion based upon your attitude from above. Functioning from above, this lady is tasting of the power of the age to come.

In the 10th chapter of Luke, the story is told of seventy disciples, who — having been sent out into the world returned thrilled beyond measure, and said: "Lord, even the demons were subject to us in your name." Then he said: "I saw Satan fall from heaven. Nevertheless, rejoice not that the spirits are subject to you, but that your names are written in heaven." I say to her, rejoice not that you have tasted of this power, but rejoice because your name is written in heaven. This is infinitely greater than demonstrating your power in this world.

Now, Luke does not speak of seventy individuals which were sent out, but the numerical value of the Hebrew letter *Ayin*,[14] whose symbolic value is the eye. This is not the outside eye, but the incurrent eye, which sees inward into the world of thought. You have the incurrent eye, nevertheless rejoice – not because the spirit was subject unto you, but because your name is written in heaven. One day when you are called into that assemblage, you will see that there is such a record, and your name is written in heaven.

This may seem stupid to the intelligent mind. That is because they are sound asleep. This Manson boy, now on trial for the murders recently committed by his group, fell into a power of which he is totally unaware. Many who became his slaves were simple people, some cultured. One had attended college for three years.

His power, exercised without love, resulted in a horrible experience; but she exercised her power in love, saying: "You don't want to kill her. You love her and she loves you." She released the man from his violent state by the power of love. This world is every bit as much a dream as that world, and you, its dreamer, are God learning to exercise your powerful imagination, in love.

You can take this message on either level. Use it as my friend did, when she would not accept the fact that her luggage was missing, or test your power from above. Scripture claims that: Whatever you desire, if you will believe you already have it, you will.

---

[14] Ayin

Refusing to believe her luggage was missing, my friend fulfilled her desire by placing it on the bed, removing its contents, and putting them away. This she did every night for five weeks, and then one day she received a notice saying that if she did not pick up her luggage within five days she would be charged storage!

I can't thank her enough for sharing this experience with me, that I may share it with you to encourage you to control your human imagination; for if you would steer a true course toward a certain goal in life, you must ever be aware of the end that you are shaping by your imaginal activity, and not allow doubt to enter for one moment. When you know what you want, you must think from your belief in its possession, morning, noon, and night. If you do, no power can stop its appearance, because you are the dreamer of your dream, pushing yourself out, shaping your world by your imaginal activities.

Your own wonderful human imagination is the Jehovah and Jesus of scripture. The words mean: "*Jehovah is salvation, or Jehovah saves.*" In the 3rd chapter of Exodus, Jehovah revealed his name as I am. You are not John or Mary, but simply I am. In the 4th chapter of the Book of Genesis we are told that when Abel (the 2nd son) was killed, Eve bore Seth, a son to take Abel's place. Seth then had a son called Enosh, "*And from that day on, men began to call upon the name of God.*"[15]

Now, the words "call upon" literally mean "call with." It is nonsense to say: "In the name of Jesus; in the name of God; or in the name of Jehovah." If you say: "In the name of Jesus

---

[15] Remember, in the lady's dream the second husband was killed.

Christ," you do not feel anything. But when you call with the name, you say: I am unpacking the suitcase. I am hanging the clothes in the closet. I am putting the presents away. I am arresting the activity within and silencing those who stand before me. I am saying: "You love her and she loves you.'" That's calling with the name of God. And from that moment on, men began to call with the name of God.

If you really believe me, you will prove my words in the testing. The two ladies have proved it and shared their experiences with me. I can't tell you my thrill when I know that you have heard me to the point of applying my words. One who is the incurrent eyewitness took it into the depth and saw into eternity. The other knows the truth, and believes it on this level of her being. From this level she brought her luggage back with all of its contents in place, while the other went into a deeper level of her being to discover that there was nothing on the outside but herself.

Mennonites are only expressions of fixations. They haven't changed their outer dress in 300 years. Satisfying their conscience, they will loan you a dollar and not accept any interest on the loan; but they can feel justified in buying land and holding it until the price goes up. You see, man has a peculiar, innate something that justifies everything he does, thereby making him pure in his own eyes.

But I say to you: your imagination manifests itself in the imaginations of men. The world is playing its part, because you are imagining every moment in time. Who knows who is treading in the winepress tonight, causing the subtle change in the minds of men. Perhaps he feels wrongfully accused, and is now sitting in jail thinking of getting even with society. That's treading in the winepress. When he can lift his thoughts to the point of vision, the act is committed, and it will manifest itself in the world of man,

Vision is simply awakening in the dream. Asleep, you seem to be the victim of your dreams; but awake, as you are here, you can become discriminating. She awoke in her dream, making it vision. Realizing that it started as a dream – therefore, it must still be a dream – she knew the people were only herself made visible, so she could change them. Placing the thought of love in the mind of the man, he became aware of his radical change of thinking, yet was totally unaware of who produced it.

Who knows who is producing the changes in the minds of men today, producing war or peace. It could be some woman treading in the winepress; or – as Yeats said – it could be in the mind of some shepherd boy, lighting up his eyes for a moment before he ran upon his way. Dreaming of heroism, of noble battles where he was the hero, that little boy can cause the blood to flow. If you know who you are and how imagination operates, you will learn to control your imaginal activities. If you do not, they will be controlled for you by another, and you will become their victim.

Any time you exercise your imagination lovingly on behalf of another you have done the right thing. But if it is not done in love there is a question mark, for God is love. This knowledge is not the result of some philosophic reasoning, but of self-revelation. God unveiled himself within me and now I know that God is Infinite love. Yes, he is Infinite Power and Wisdom as well, but power without love can raise horror.

I say to everyone, believe me. The Jesus of scripture and the Jehovah of scripture are your own wonderful human imagination. There is no other God, and God is love. One day you will know this truth, but in the meanwhile believe me as the lady did. When her natural human impulse was to curse, she blessed by imagining her luggage on her bed. Then she performed in her imagination what she would do in the flesh if her desire was now outpictured on her screen of space. This world is a play, peopled by those in costumes. You are its author, writing your play. You can change it (as my friend did) and prove to yourself that you can take a fixed idea (symbolized as a Mennonite) and change it.

Believe me, imagining does create reality. Take me seriously. You will never know Jesus until you know the secret of imagining, for your imagination is he. If you really believe in God, believe in your own imagination, for it is the power of God and the wisdom of God. The power and wisdom of the lady's imaginal act influenced the entire outer world and produced that so-called "lost" bag and returned it.

I tell you, there is only one power in the universe. We call it by the name of God or Jesus. But if you think of Jesus as someone on the outside, who lived 2,000 years ago, you will never know him. Nor will you ever know God, if you think of him as some impersonal force. God is a person because you are a person. He became you, as he became us all, that we may become as He is.

Take my message to heart and apply it from now on. You can be the man you would like to be. Don't start dreaming about it. Awake and think from it. Do not concern yourself about trying to meet the so-called "right" people. They are simply reflections of the activity you have placed within you. Change your thoughts and you will change the behavior of those who surround you for they are nothing more than yourself made visible.

The day will come when you will awake from this dream, and you will see what my friend saw in another aspect of the dream – that the world is dead, and only the reflection of an activity of the human imagination. Then you will depart, leaving the world as it is for others to play upon, while you return to the being you really are – the Lord God Himself, the creator of the dream.

Now let us go into the silence.

The Secret *of* Prayer

he secret of scriptural prayer, as told in the form of a parable, is to pray and never lose heart. One such parable tells of a widow who kept coming to a judge, asking for vindication. At first he did not respond, then he said to himself: "Although I neither fear God, nor regard man, yet I will exonerate her, because by her much coming, she wearies me." Parables, like dreams, contain a single jet of truth. This parable urges persistence in mastering the art of prayer. Once you have mastered it you will live in the state of thanksgiving, and all through the day you will say over and over again to yourself: "Thank you, Father."

A most effective prayer is found in the 11th chapter of the Book of John, as: "*Father, I thank thee that thou hast heard me, for thou always hears me.*" In this chapter, the story is told of someone who has died and has seemingly gone from this world. But the truth is that no one is dead to you, when you know how to pray. You may no longer touch, see, or hear those you love with your mortal senses; but if you know how to give thanks, you can move from your body of darkness into the world of light and encounter your loved ones there. Therefore, he who would learn how to pray will discover the great secret of a full and happy life.

In the 33rd chapter of the Book of Genesis, Jerusalem is called "Shechem." It is said that, "Jacob came safely into the city of Shechem, which is in the land of Canaan. There he erected an altar and called it El Elohey Israel, which means "the God of Israel". Orienting himself toward Shechem (the true direction) Jacob remained in El Elohey Israel, which means "safe in mind, body, or estate".

We are told that Daniel oriented himself at an open window, where he looked toward Jerusalem. And those in the Mohammedan world pray looking towards what they call Mecca. But because Christianity takes place within, scripture is speaking of the Jerusalem within, and not on the outside at all. When you pray you do not prostrate yourself on the ground and look towards some eastern point in space, but adjust yourself mentally into your fulfilled desire. Although this technique is simple, it takes practice to become its master. Your true direction is to the knowledge of what you want. Knowing your desire, point yourself directly in front of it by thinking from its fulfillment. Silence all thought and allow the doors of your mind to open. Then enter your desire. Stay with your imagination as your companion. Start by thinking of your imagination as something other than yourself, and eventually you will know you are what you formerly called your imagination. It is possible to amputate a hand, leg, or various parts of the body – but imagination cannot be amputated, for it is your eternal Self!

Let me show you what I mean. While standing here in Los Angeles, I may desire to be elsewhere. Time and finances may not allow it, but in my imagination I can assume I am already there. Now, by a mere act of assumption on my part, God departs this body. If I assume I am in New York City, anyone I think of in Los Angeles must be three thousand miles away.

No longer can I think of them as just down the street or in the hills west of me. That is my test.

The word "prayer" means "motion towards, accession to, act or in the vicinity of". Orienting myself towards New York City, I have made a motion, an accession to. As I act in the vicinity of, I see my friends relative to New York City. Having done this, let me have full confidence in my imagination, knowing he is the being who made the motion. Blake's words are true: "Man is all Imagination, and God is Man and exists in us and we in Him. Man's Immortal Body is the Imagination, and that is God Himself."

You can not only move in space but also in time and fulfill your every desire. Prayer does not have to be confined to what a person calls self. You can pray for another by feeling they now have what they formerly wanted, for feeling is a movement. The first creative act recorded in scripture is motion: "God moved upon the face of the water."

A friend recently had a fantastic vision, during which he asked: "Did I learn anything?" and I answered: "Yes. You learned how to move." Then everything was transformed, as conflict deceased, a hovel became a castle, the battlefield a sea of ripened wheat, and he was escorted into his eternal home. Prayer is motion. It is learning how to move toward a change in your bank balance, your marital status, or social world. Learn to master the art of motion; for after you move, change begins to rise up out of the deep. The technique of prayer is mastering your inner motion. If you are seeing things you would like to change, move in your imagination to the position you would occupy after the change took place.

Everything and everyone in your world is yourself pushed out. Any request from another – heard by you – should not be ignored; for it is coming from yourself! You came down from a world of light to confine yourself to this body of darkness. Now a spark from an infinite world of light, one day you will remember that world and awaken, but in the meantime you must learn to exercise the power of your mind. Having remembered the infinite world of light, I now know that everything is myself, as all things are contained within me.

Prayer is psychological movement. It is the art of moving from a problem to its solution. When a friend calls, telling of a problem, we hang up, and I move from the problem state to its solution by hearing the same lady tell me the problem is now solved.

A friend recently shared this dream with me: We were in a garden and he told me all of his desires, when I said: "Don't desire them, live them!" This is true. Desire is thinking of! Living is thinking from! Don't go through life desiring. Live your desire. Think it is already fulfilled. Believe it is true; for an assumption, though false, if persisted in will harden into fact.

When you are learning the art of prayer, persistence is necessary, as told us in the story of the man who – coming at night – said: "Friend, lend me three loaves of bread." Although his friend replied: "It is late, the door is closed, my children are in bed, and I cannot come down and serve you," because of the man's importunity, his friend gave him what he wanted. The word importunity means brazen impudence. The man repeated and repeated his request, unwilling to take no for an answer. The same is true in the story of the widow. These are all parables told to illustrate prayer.

The Lord's Prayer teaches the oneness of us all. It begins: "Our Father." If God is our Father, are we not one? Regardless of our race or color of skin, if we have a common Father, we must have a common brotherhood.

Eventually we are all going to know we are the Father; but in the meanwhile, persistence is the key to a change in life – more income, greater recognition, or whatever the desire may be. If your desire is not fulfilled today, tomorrow, next week or next month – persist, for persistency will pay off. All of your prayers will be answered if you will not give up.

My old friend, Abdullah, gave me this exercise. Every day I would sit in my living room where I could not see the telephone in the hall. With my eyes closed, I would assume I was in the chair by the phone. Then I would feel myself back in the living room. This I did over and over again, as I discovered the feeling of changing motion. This exercise was very helpful to me. If you try it, you will discover you become very loose with this exercise.

Practice the art of motion, and one day you will discover that by the very act of imagining, you are detached from your physical body and placed exactly where you are imagining yourself to be – so much so that you are seen by those who are there.

Being all imagination, you must be wherever you are in imagination. Moving in your imagination, you are preparing a place for your desires to be fulfilled. Then you return, to walk through a series of events which will lead you up to where you have placed yourself. In imagination, I can put myself where I desire to be. I move and view the world from there. Then I return here, confident that – in a way unknown to me – this being who can do all things and knows all things, will lead me physically across a bridge of incident up to where I have placed myself. You can move in imagination to any place and any time. Dwell there as though it were true, and you will have learned the secret of prayer.

My wife had a wonderful vision where she found herself in a grove of trees. Walking down a clear passage, she saw people gathered around an altar. A lady approached, carrying a book entitled, The Credence of Faith and the Forgiveness of Sins according to Judaism. Reaching the altar, she began to read it aloud. Shortly, another lady appeared, carrying a book entitled, The Credence of Faith and the Forgiveness of Sins according to Christianity. Approaching the altar, she too opened her book and began to read. As my wife listened, she realized it was infinitely more difficult to be a Christian than to be a Jew. She saw the whole thing was psychological. That nothing is done on the outside, because everything comes from within.

Browning began his wonderful poem, "Easter Day" with the words: "How hard it is to be a Christian." And Chapman said: "Christianity has not been tried and proved wanting. It has been tried and found difficult and therefore given up." Why? *Because a Christian cannot pass the buck and blame another.* Christianity is built upon the foundation that all are one. That man is forever drawing conformation of what he is doing within himself. That your world bears witness to what you are doing to yourself. This is difficult to accept, yet it is Christianity. No man comes unto me, save my Father who sent me calls him. I and my Father are one, therefore I call all those who enter my life to reveal to me what I am doing in my imagination.

Learn how to pray. Master it and make your world conform to the ideal you want to experience. Stop thinking of, and start thinking from. To think from the wish fulfilled is to realize that which you will never experience while you are thinking of it. When you put yourself into the state of the wish fulfilled and think from it, you are praying, and in a way your reasoning mind does not know, your wish will become a fact in your world. You can be the man or woman you want to be, when you know how to pray. All things are possible to him who believes, therefore learn the art of believing and persuade yourself it is true. Then one day, occupying space and time in your imagination, you will be seen by another, who will call or send you a letter verifying your visit. This I know from experience.

The Bible is not just beautiful poetry; it is the inspired word of God. Written by poets, they have given enlarged meaning to normal words. When you put your body on the bed and assume you are elsewhere, are you not all imagination? In the act of imagining, you depart the dark caverns of this body and appear where you imagine yourself to be, because you are God – all imagination – and cannot die. You cannot go to eternal death in that which cannot die, and your immortal being is imagination! You are the central being of scripture – the one called Jesus Christ, who is the Lord God Jehovah – who descended here for a purpose.

While here, you must pay the price of living in the world of Caesar. You may criticize our politicians and protest any raise in taxes, but you will continue to be taxed. All you have to do is learn the art of prayer and make more money.

I am reminded of a story told of the late President Kennedy. It seems his father – who had, in one generation, made something like four-hundred million dollars – complained that his children were spending too much money. At a banquet, President Kennedy said: "The only solution to this problem is for father to make more money."

One day a friend told me that when she was a child, her father would say: "If you have but a dollar and it was necessary for you to spend it, do so as if it were a dry leaf, and you the owner of a boundless forest." If one really knows how to pray, he could spend his dollar and then reproduce it again. You see, this world is brought into being by man's imagination, so it is very important to learn the secret of prayer.

If you are still desiring, stop it right now! Ask yourself what it would be like, were your desire a reality. How would you feel if you were already the one you would like to be? The moment you catch that mood, you are thinking from it. And the great secret of prayer is thinking from, rather than thinking of. Anchored here, you know where you live, your bank balance, job, creditors, friends, and loved ones – as you are thinking from this state. But you can move to another state and give it the same sense of reality, when you find and practice the great secret of prayer.

Take my message to heart and live by it. Practice the art of prayer daily, and then one day you will find the most effective prayer is: "Thank you Father." You will feel this being within you as your very self. You can speak of it as "thou" yet know it is "I." You will then have a thou/I relationship, and say to yourself: "Thank you, Father". If I want something, I know the desire comes from the Father, because all thought springs from Him. Having given me the urge, I thank Him for fulfilling it. Then I walk by faith, in confidence that he who gave it to me through the medium of desire will clothe it in bodily form for me to encounter in the flesh.

Don't get in the habit of judging and criticizing, seeing only unlovely things. You have a life – live it nobly. It is so much easier to be noble, generous, loving, and kind, than to be judgmental. If others want to do so, let them.

They are an aspect of yourself that you haven't overcome yet, but don't fall into that habit. Simply thank your heavenly Father over and over and over again, because in the end, when the curtain comes down on this wonderful drama, the supreme actor will rise from it all and you will know that you are He.

Now let us go into the silence.

CPSIA information can be obtained
at www.ICGtesting.com
Printed in the USA
BVOW08s1159270817

492868BV00001B/214/P

9 781603 866750